RABBIT PALS

Crabtree Publishing Company
www.crabtreebooks.com
1-800-387-7650

Published in Canada
Crabtree Publishing
616 Welland Avenue
St. Catharines, ON
L2M 5V6

Published in the United States
Crabtree Publishing
PMB 59051
350 Fifth Ave, 59th Floor
New York, NY 10118

Published in 2018 by CRABTREE PUBLISHING COMPANY.

First published in 2017 by Wayland
Copyright © Hodder and Stoughton, 2017

Author: Pat Jacobs

Editor: Elizabeth Brent

Project coordinator: Kathy Middleton

Editor: Petrice Custance

Cover and Interior Design: Dynamo

Proofreader: Wendy Scavuzzo

Prepress technician: Samara Parent

Print and production coordinator: Margaret Amy Salter

Photographs:
iStock: Eric Isselée; p2 tyler olson, UroshPetrovic, SurkovDimitri; p3 Dorottya_Mathe; p4 GlobalP; p6 Eric Isselée, Julia Mashkova, matooker, GlobalP; p7 Susan Schmitz, GlobalP, Eric Isselée; p8 chengyuzheng, 5second, Dorottya_Mathe, Erik Lam; p9 suemack, indavostrovska, MGStockPhotography, Craig Dingle; p10 chengyuzheng; p11 &#169 CJKPhoto; p12 Elgars Retigs; p13 XiXinXing, gurinaleksandr; p14 &#169 Norman Chan, -slav-, Toshiro Shimada; p15 SeashoreDesign, Stefano Tinti; p16 Bronwyn8, vydrin; p17 Silke Dietze, baramee2554, GlobalP, kali9; p18 Marco Hegner, Nikolay Suslov; p19 Ramaboin, coramueller; p20 Phillip Danze, photobac; p21 wzooff, Dmitry Ersler, gutaper; p22 Elgars Retigs; p23 photosaint, lindavostrovska, bazilfoto, cynoclub; p24 Murmakova, chengyuzheng; p25 GlobalP; p26 Milos Stojanovic, FtLaudGirl, justtscott, William Attard McCarthy, Voren1, ALEXIUZ; p27 AnikaSalsera, akiyoko, feedough, Marina Maslennikova; p28 Voren1, Eric Isselée; p29 Stefan Petru Andronache; p32 CPaulussen; Front cover : Eric Isselée; Back cover: iava777

Shutterstock: p5 tr Imageman; p10 c Stephen Rees; p17 cl Goldfinch4ever; p24 Samuel Borges Photography

Alamy: p10 Janet Horton; p12 ableimages; p25 Arco Images GmbH

Every attempt has been made to clear copyright. Should there be any inadvertent omission, please apply to the publisher for rectification. The website addresses (URLs) included in this book were valid at the time of going to press. However, it is possible that contents or addresses may have changed since the publication of this book. No responsibility for any such changes can be accepted by either the author or the Publisher.

Printed in the USA / 072017 / CG20170524

Library and Archives Canada Cataloguing in Publication

Jacobs, Pat, author
  Rabbit pals / Pat Jacobs.

(Pet pals)
Includes index.
Issued in print and electronic formats.
ISBN 978-0-7787-3561-8 (hardcover).--
ISBN 978-0-7787-3583-0 (softcover).--
ISBN 978-1-4271-1948-3 (HTML)

  1. Rabbits--Juvenile literature. 2. Rabbits--Behavior--Juvenile literature. I. Title.

SF453.2.J33 2017   j636.932'2   C2017-902523-6
                                              C2017-902524-4

Library of Congress Cataloging-in-Publication Data

Names: Jacobs, Pat, author.
Title: Rabbit pals / Pat Jacobs.
Description: New York, New York : Crabtree Publishing, 2018. |
  Series: Pet pals | Audience: Age 7-10. | Audience: Grade K to 3.
  | Includes index.
Identifiers: LCCN 2017016727 (print) | LCCN 2017027437 (ebook)
  ISBN 9781427119483 (Electronic HTML) |
  ISBN 9780778735618 (reinforced library binding) |
  ISBN 9780778735830 (pbk.)
Subjects: LCSH: Rabbits--Juvenile literature.
Classification: LCC SF453.2 (ebook) | LCC SF453.2 .J33 2018 (print)
  | DDC 636.932/2--dc23
LC record available at https://lccn.loc.gov/2017016727

CONTENTS

Your rabbit from head to tail   **4**

Bunny breeds   **6**

Choosing your rabbit   **8**

Home sweet home!   **10**

Making friends   **12**

Rabbit rations   **14**

Day-to-day care   **16**

Health and safety   **18**

Bunny behavior   **20**

Communication   **22**

Training   **24**

Fun and games   **26**

Rabbit quiz   **28**

Quiz answers   **30**

Learning more   **31**

Glossary & Index   **32**

YOUR RABBIT
FROM HEAD TO TAIL

Rabbits make great pets and each one has its own personality—they can be as playful as puppies and as mischievous as kittens. Rabbits are sociable creatures and enjoy spending time with people, but they need a bunny buddy, too.

Eyes: Rabbits' eyes are high up on the sides of their head. They can see in every direction and spot **predators** approaching from behind and above.

Tail: Rabbits sometimes wag their tail when they are annoyed or don't want to do as you ask.

Hind legs: Rabbits' long, strong hind legs allow them to stand up tall to look for predators, and to run fast to escape them.

Ears: The shape of rabbits' ears allows them to hear sounds more than 2 miles (3.2 km) away. They can also hear high-pitched sounds that humans can't.

Whiskers: A bunny's whiskers are the width of its body, so they warn the rabbit if it is about to enter a narrow tunnel where it could get stuck.

Teeth: Rabbits' teeth never stop growing, but they are worn down by chewing on tough plants.

Nose: Rabbits have a great sense of smell, as well as extra scent organs in the roof of their mouth. This helps them to detect predators before they see them.

RABBIT FACTS

- Rabbits can run at speeds of up to 30 miles (48.3 km) an hour.

- The world's biggest rabbit is named Darius. He is 4.4 feet (1.3 m) long and weighs 49 pounds (22.2 kg)!

Paws: The bottoms of rabbits' feet are padded with fur to cushion them.

BUNNY BREEDS

Rabbits range in size from the cute little Netherland Dwarf, which is about the size of a guinea pig, to giant **breeds** that grow as large as a medium-sized dog. Here are a few of the most popular breeds:

Rex rabbits have a thick, velvety coat that is lovely to stroke. They make good house rabbits and are said to have a cat-like personality.

Dwarf Lop rabbits have wide ears that hang down beside their head. They are friendly and playful, and enjoy being with people and other rabbits.

Dutch rabbits have a V-shaped white patch on their face and a white front. They are gentle, friendly, and intelligent so they make great pets.

English Spot rabbits are medium-sized with a white coat and colored markings. They are lively, inquisitive pets that need plenty of exercise.

Harlequin rabbits are gentle, curious pets that enjoy playing and like to be the center of attention. They need a lot of space and can live inside or outside.

Angora rabbits are covered in long hair, which means they need grooming every day. For this reason, they are not the best choice for a busy family.

Flemish Giant rabbits are one of the largest breeds, and grow about as large as a medium-sized dog. They are good-natured and get along with other pets, so they make great house bunnies.

Belgian Hares are rabbits, despite their name. They have a long, slim body and long legs and ears. They are one of the most energetic and intelligent breeds.

CHOOSING YOUR RABBIT

In the wild, rabbits live in groups. It's best to get at least two rabbits, otherwise your bunny will be lonely. Before you buy or adopt a rabbit, check that its eyes are sparkling, its teeth meet up properly at the front, and its ears are clean.

BABY ADULT?

Baby bunnies are adorable, but they can be destructive and it can be hard to tell if they are male or female. By choosing an adult, you can find out about your new pet's personality and, if you get one from a rescue center, it will have been health-checked and **spayed** or **neutered**.

LONG- 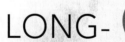 SHORT-HAIRED?

Long-haired rabbits are cute bundles of fur, but they are high-maintenance pets. While short-haired bunnies need grooming about once a week, long-haired rabbits must be brushed every day, or their fur will get matted and their skin may tear.

LARGE **OR** SMALL?

Giant bunnies make great pets, if you have the space for them. They will need to live in the house or in a shed with a large run. Dwarf rabbits are easier to handle and live up to three times longer, but they still need plenty of space to exercise.

MALE **OR** FEMALE?

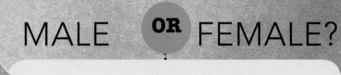

Unneutered male rabbits spray urine, and unspayed females can be very **territorial**, but both make great pets once they have been neutered or spayed.

INDOOR **OR** OUTDOOR RABBIT?

Rabbits make good house pets, if you bunny-proof your home. You'll be able to spend more time with them and they will probably get more exercise than they would in an outdoor run. Outdoor rabbits need a large, predator-proof cage and run.

HOME SWEET HOME!

Your rabbit needs a clean, safe hutch to live in, where it can eat, sleep, rest, and hide if it feels scared. It also needs plenty of room to hop, run, jump, and stretch out for a snooze. Here's how to create the perfect pad for your bunny:

Your rabbit needs room to stretch out, and to stand up on its back legs without touching the ceiling.

Line the sleeping area with newspaper and fresh hay.

A lock will keep your pets safe inside.

PET CHECK ☑

Does your bunny have:

- enough room?
- a safe exercise run?
- its own food bowl?
- a water bowl or bottle?
- clean bedding?

PET TALK

Please put me in my run for a hop in the early morning and late afternoon. That's when I am feeling most active!

KEEP IT CLEAN!

- Clean out the toilet area every day
- Clean out the hutch once a week
- Only use pet-safe cleaning products

Line the eating area with newspaper and wood shavings.

Line a toilet area with newspaper and wood shavings. Be sure to set it up away from the sleeping area.

Choose a hutch with a mesh door to let in fresh air.

Your rabbit will need a place to exercise. This can be an outdoor or indoor run, or a rabbit-proofed room in your home.

MAKING FRIENDS

The best way to get to know your new friend is by sitting quietly on the floor. Rabbits are naturally friendly and **inquisitive**, so if you hold out a treat, such as a piece of carrot, your bunny will probably come to you.

Give your bunny a chance to get used to the sounds and smells of its new home before you try to play with it. Rabbits are quite timid – they need to know they have a safe place to hide if they get scared because they are **prey** to many animals.

Play gently alongside your new pet. Most rabbits prefer not to be picked up or held. Let them show you what they like.

TAKE IT SLOWLY

Rabbits can't see very clearly, and they have a **blind spot** in front of their nose. They may get frightened if you approach them suddenly, especially from behind, because this is what a predator would do.

HOW TO STROKE YOUR BUNNY

Most rabbits like being stroked on the forehead and around the shoulders. They may not like being touched on the ears, feet, stomach, or tail.

PET TALK

My favorite companion is another rabbit. Predators, such as cats and dogs, are not my natural friends, and I may bully guinea pigs.

OTHER PETS

Make sure your new rabbit is safe inside a cage before introducing other pets, and don't leave them alone together unless you know they will not hurt each other.

RABBIT RATIONS

A rabbit's main food should be good-quality hay. Chewing on hay wears its teeth down so they don't grow too long.

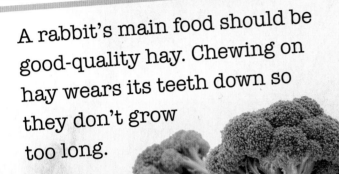

SPECIAL TREATS

Rabbits love fresh vegetables, but if they have too many they won't eat their hay (which keeps them healthy) and they may get diarrhea. Leafy vegetables, carrots, and broccoli make good bunny treats, but they should never have peas, beans, corn, rhubarb leaves, potatoes, onions, or garlic.

STRANGE, BUT TRUE

Because wild rabbits have to survive on poor-quality grass, they eat some of their droppings to get as much goodness from their food as possible. These special soft droppings are usually produced at night. You may see your rabbit eating them directly from its bottom.

WATER

A rabbit needs as much water as a medium-sized dog. A water bottle with a metal spout is better than a bowl of water, which can get dirty or be knocked over.

WEIGHT WATCHING

Pet rabbits are not as active as those in the wild, so if they eat too many treats they can easily put on weight. An overweight rabbit can't groom itself properly, which can lead to health problems.

DAILY DIET ☑

Each day, your rabbit should have:

- a bundle of hay the size of its body
- a handful of fresh greens
- 1 tbsp (15 ml) green rabbit pellets

When you stroke your bunny, you should be able to feel its spine and ribs.

DAY-TO-DAY CARE

Checking on your rabbit every day is the most important part of being a good pet owner. You should make sure its droppings look normal, that it is eating and drinking, and that it doesn't seem unwell, or in pain.

Your vet can trim your rabbit's teeth and claws if they get too long.

GROOMING

Rabbits groom themselves and their friends, but if they swallow a lot of hair it can get stuck in their stomach and cause a serious problem. That's why it's important to brush a short-haired bunny every week and a long-haired rabbit every day.

TEETH AND CLAWS

Keep an eye on your rabbit's teeth and claws to make sure they're not getting overgrown. If its teeth get too long, your bunny won't be able to eat. Pet rabbits may not wear their claws down enough, especially if they live indoors, and overgrown claws can get ripped out.

Please be gentle when you brush my coat because I have very delicate skin.

PESKY PARASITES

Rabbits may pick up **parasites** such as **fleas** and **ticks**, so check for signs of them when grooming your bunny. Look inside its ears as well, in case your pet has ear **mites**.

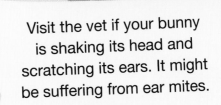

Visit the vet if your bunny is shaking its head and scratching its ears. It might be suffering from ear mites.

BATH BAN

Rabbits don't like getting wet and shouldn't be given a bath because they will panic and may injure themselves. If your bunny gets dirty, it's best to spot-clean the area with a little water and some pet shampoo.

FLIES

If rabbits have dirty fur, perhaps because they have diarrhea or are too old or overweight to clean themselves properly, flies may lay their eggs on them, which can cause infection or disease. Be sure to check your rabbit's fur every day, especially during the summer months.

HEALTH AND SAFETY

Rabbits may be attacked by dogs, cats, foxes, weasels, badgers, and some birds, so make sure their cages and runs are secure. Rabbits thump the ground with their back legs if they sense a predator nearby, so if you hear that sound, check that your pet is safe.

INDOOR HAZARDS

It's a bunny's **instinct** to chew, so you'll need to rabbit-proof your home by lifting any cables out of reach, or covering them with strong plastic tubing. An electric shock could kill your pet.

It's best to play with your bunny at ground level and let an adult pick it up if necessary, because rabbits can break their spines if they fall.

NEUTERING

Getting your rabbits neutered or spayed makes them more friendly and well behaved, and it protects them from many health problems. It also helps for a calmer homelife, as an unspayed female rabbit can have more than 70 babies in just one year! Don't forget—rabbits can start making babies at just 10 weeks old.

VACCINATIONS

Your pet can catch deadly diseases from wild rabbits and insects. There are no cures for many of these diseases, so it is very important to **vaccinate** your bunny against them.

PET TALK

Please remember I'm wearing a fur coat. Keep my cage in the shade in summer, and please don't leave me in a hot room.

POISONOUS PLANTS

Common plants that are poisonous for rabbits include bindweed, buttercups, elder, foxgloves, ivy, lupins, laburnum, oak leaves, privet, and rhubarb, as well as apple seeds and many types of wood. Search online for a full list.

BUNNY BEHAVIOR

In the wild, rabbits explore the world by sniffing, nudging, chewing, and digging. They are often mischievous and curious, and they don't give up easily!

CHEWING AND DIGGING

Chewing and digging are part of a rabbit's natural behavior, so you can't blame them for trying to chew through the table leg or dig up the floor. It's best to give them toys they can chew, and a sandpit or box full of shredded paper so they can behave naturally without causing damage.

SCENT-MARKING

Rabbits have scent **glands** under their chins, so your bunny may rub its chin against things to **scent-mark** what it considers part of its territory – which could include you.

BUNNY BINKIES

If your rabbit jumps in the air like a jack-in-the-box, twists its body and flicks its head and feet, it's performing a "binky." This means you have a very happy bunny.

BORED BUNNY

If a rabbit starts grooming itself more often than usual it could be a sign of boredom, especially if it lives alone. A bored rabbit may also chew its cage and throw its toys or food bowl around.

NOSE TWITCHING

Rabbits are well known for twitching their noses. It's a sign of how interested they are in what's going on. If there's a lot of activity nearby, their nose may twitch at great speed. When it's quieter and they are relaxed, this will slow down or stop.

PET TALK

I have an extra, clear eyelid. Sometimes when I'm asleep, I close it and I look as though I'm sleeping with my eyes open.

COMMUNICATION

Rabbits make their feelings known through their ears, tail, **body language**, and the noises they make. Here's a guide to what your bunny is trying to tell you:

BUNNY BODY LANGUAGE

When a rabbit is happy and relaxed, it will flop down on to its side or roll on to its back with its eyes closed. If your bunny is feeling friendly, it will face you and may even give you a nudge. But if you've done something to upset it, it will turn its back. You can try doing the same if your rabbit does something you don't like!

BUNNY CHAT

Some rabbits have a lot to say, while others are fairly quiet. Here are some examples of bunny noises and what they mean:

- **Soft tooth grinding:** I'm happy.

- **Chattering teeth or loud tooth grinding:** I'm in pain.

- **Muttering:** I'm angry or unhappy.

- **Growling or hissing:** I'm very angry.

- **Squealing:** I'm in pain or very frightened.

- **Clucking:** I'm relaxed.

PET TALK

If I suddenly become aggressive or start hiding, I may be ill or in pain.

BEWARE!

An angry rabbit will growl or grunt and may flick its tail from side to side. This could be a warning that it's getting ready to bite, so it's best to back off.

EXPRESSIVE EARS

The position of a rabbit's ears is a clue to how it's feeling.

- **Flicking ears:** I want to play.

- **Ears up and turned forward:** I'm happy.

- **Ears turning sideways, then backward:** I'm getting annoyed.

- **Ears tilted forward:** I'm curious.

- **Ears tilted far back:** I'm angry so leave me alone.

- **Ears lowered and facing downward:** I'm very unhappy and might be ill.

TRAINING

Training your rabbit is fun for you both. Always use treats to reward your bunny when it does as you ask. Never punish it for doing the wrong thing because your rabbit will become afraid of you. Clicker training is a good way to start.

CLICKER TRAINING

Cat-training clickers might be too loud for your rabbit, so try using a ballpoint pen. Click the pen, wait for a second, then give your bunny a treat. Move farther away and click the pen again, then give your rabbit a treat if it comes to you. Repeat this several times.

HERE, BUNNY!

Once your rabbit comes to you when it hears the clicker, start calling its name after each click before handing over the treat. Repeat this several times, then try calling without the clicker to see if your rabbit comes to you when it hears its name.

HOME TIME

Training your rabbit to go back into its cage or carrier will save you from having to catch it. Sit close to the cage and use the clicker to call your pet, then put a treat inside. Repeat this several times while calling, "Home!" Then try this without the clicker.

LITTER TRAINING

Put a layer of newspaper in a shallow tray and cover it with hay, or litter suitable for rabbits (not cat litter). Scoop up a few droppings and scatter them in the tray to encourage your bunny to use it.

If your rabbit leaves droppings in a different part of the room or enclosure, move the tray there.

TRAINING TIPS

- Only have one animal in the room during training.

- There should be no noise except the clicker and your voice.

- Training should only last a few minutes.

- Make sure your bunny has mastered one trick before moving on to the next.

- If your rabbit isn't interested, stop and try again later.

PET TALK

I'm quite clever! I can learn to jump through a hoop and to roll a ball.

FUN AND GAMES

Rabbits are very active animals and need at least three hours of exercise every day. They love to play, so try some of these games and activities to see which your bunny likes best.

Stuff a paper towel roll tube with hay and hide a treat inside for your bunny to find.

THROWING TOYS

Rabbits like toys they can hold in their mouths and throw around, but don't expect them to play "fetch." You will be the one who has to get the toy.

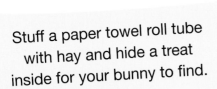

TOPPLING TOYS

Most rabbits like to knock things over, so set up some plastic bottles, a pyramid of balls, or a pile of plastic bricks, then let your bunny loose.

Remove any parcel tape and staples from boxes.

MAKE A RABBIT PLAY AREA

Create a cardboard city using boxes, tubes, and tunnels, and include a box full of shredded paper for digging. Cut windows and doors in the large boxes and add some toys, such as balls with bells inside, for extra bunny fun.

WHEN TO PLAY

Rabbits are most active in the early morning and early evening, so this is the best time to play with them. When your bunny gets to know you, it will come and tell you that it wants to play by circling round your feet or pulling at your clothes.

RABBIT QUIZ

How much do you know about your rabbit pal? Take this quiz to find out.

1 Which of these rabbits is the size of a medium dog?

a. English Spot
b. Belgian Hare
c. Flemish Giant

4 Why do rabbits rub their chins against things?

a. To scent-mark them
b. To scratch their chins
c. Because they are bored

2 Which of these rabbits has long hair?

a. Angora
b. Harlequin
c. Rex

5 How often should you groom a short-haired rabbit?

a. Every day
b. Every week
c. Every month

3 How often should you clean out your rabbit's hutch?

a. Every day
b. Every week
c. Every month

Which of these vegetables is not suitable for rabbits?

a. Carrots
b. Broccoli
c. Onions

How is a rabbit feeling if its ears are tilted forward?

a. Happy
b. Curious
c. Angry

Which of these plants is bad for rabbits?

a. Buttercups
b. Grass
c. Dandelions

What is a "binky"?

a. A baby bunny
b. A rabbit toy
c. A happy jump

When are rabbits most active?

a. At night
b. Early morning and late afternoon
c. At lunchtime

QUIZ ANSWERS

1 Which of these rabbits is the size of a medium dog?

c. Flemish Giant

2 Which of these rabbits has long hair?

a. Angora

3 How often should you clean out your rabbit's hutch?

b. Every week

4 Why do rabbits rub their chins against things?

a. To scent-mark them

5 How often should you groom a short-haired rabbit?

b. Every week

6 Which of these vegetables is not suitable for rabbits?

c. Onions

7 Which of these plants is bad for rabbits?

a. Buttercups

8 What is a "binky"?

c. A happy jump

9 When are rabbits most active?

b. Early morning and late afternoon

10 How is a rabbit feeling if its ears are tilted forward?

b. Curious

LEARNING MORE

BOOKS

Ganeri, Anita. *Bunny's Guide to Caring for Your Rabbit*. Heinemann-Raintree, 2013.

Johnson, Samantha. *How to Raise Rabbits*. Voyageur Press, 2009.

MacAulay, Kelley, and Bobbie Kalman. *Rabbits*. Crabtree Publishing Company, 2005.

WEBSITES

http://pbskids.org/itsmylife/family/pets/article7.html
Check out this site for fun pet facts and great tips on caring for your rabbit.

www.lovethatpet.com/small-pets/rabbits/
This website is full of helpful information about bunny care.

http://myhouserabbit.com
Visit this site for all kinds of tips on how to be the best pal to your rabbit.

GLOSSARY

blind spot An area that can't be seen

body language Communicating through gestures and body movement

breed A group of animals with the same ancestors and characteristics

fleas Blood-sucking insects that cause itching and may carry disease

glands Organs that make fluids and chemicals, such as saliva, tears, and scent

inquisitive Curious

instinct Natural behavior that is automatic and not learned

mite A tiny creature similar to a spider

neuter An operation that stops male animals from being able to make babies

parasite A creature that lives in or on another creature and also feeds off it

predator An animal that hunts and eats other animals

prey An animal that is hunted and killed by others

scent-mark When an animal releases an odor or substance, such as urine, to mark their territory

spay An operation that stops female animals from being able to have babies

territorial When an animal claims an area for itself and defends it against intruders

tick A small, round parasite that feeds on blood

vaccinate To inject with medicine that protect animals and humans from serious diseases

INDEX

Aggression 23
Angora rabbits 7

Behavior 20–21, 22–23, 27
Belgian Hares 7
Binkies 20
Blind spot 12
Body language 22–23
Boredom 21
Breeds 6–7

Chewing 18, 20
Claws 16
Clicker training 24–25
Communication 22–23

Diet 14–15
Digging 20
Drinking 15
Dutch rabbits 6

Dwarf rabbits 6, 9

Ears 5, 13, 17, 23
Electric cables 18
English Spot rabbits 6
Eyes 4, 8, 21

Feeding 14–15
Feet 5
Fleas 17
Flemish Giant rabbits 7
Flies 17

Giant rabbits 5, 6, 7, 9
Grooming 8, 16–17, 21

Harlequin rabbits 7
Hay 10, 14, 15
Health 15, 18
House rabbits 6, 7, 9
Hutches 10, 11

Legs 4
Litter training 25

Mites 17

Netherland Dwarf rabbits 6
Neutering 8, 9, 18
Noses 5, 21

Other pets 7, 13

Parasites 17
Paws 5
Play 26–27
Poisonous plants 19
Predators 13, 18

Rex rabbits 6
Runs 11

Scent-marking 20

Sense of smell 5, 18
Sleeping 21
Spaying 8, 9, 18
Stroking 13

Tails 4
Teeth 5, 16, 22
Ticks 17
Toys 26–27
Training 24–25

Vaccinations 19
Vegetables 14
Vision 4, 12

Water 15
Weight 15
Whiskers 5